Who is Jesus?

Written by
MaryAnn Diorio, PhD, MFA

Illustrated by
Kim Sponaugle

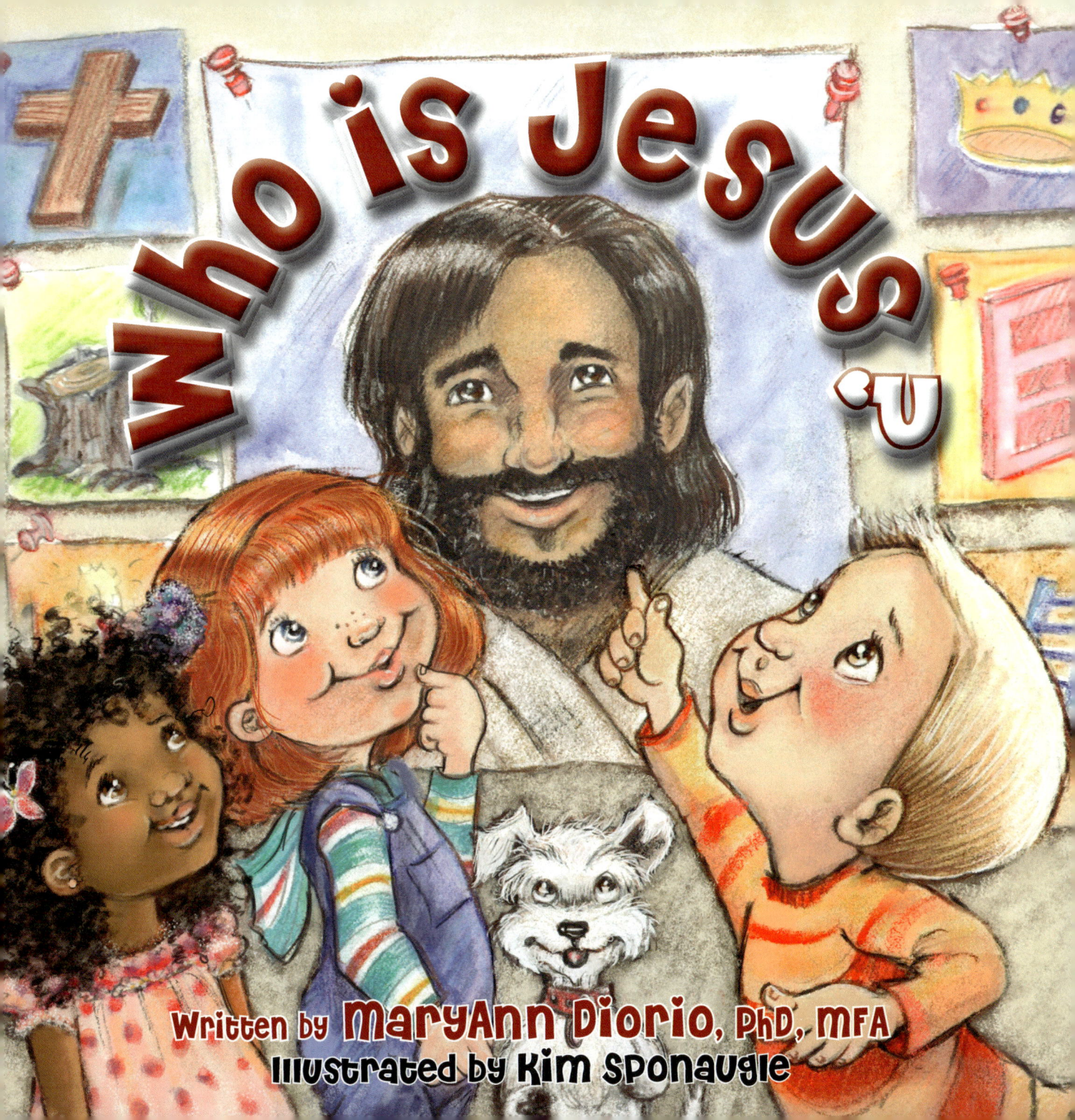

Who Is Jesus?

Copyright © 2014 MaryAnn Diorio, PhD, MFA

ISBN 978-0-930037-14-7

Library of Congress Control Number : 2014917283

From the TopNotch Press children's line

Published by TopNotch Press
PO Box 1185, Merchantville, NJ 08109
P: 856-488-3580 - F: 856-488-0291
www.topnotchpress.com
info@topnotchpress.com

Illustrated by Kim Sponaugle

Scripture is taken from Holy Bible. New Living Translation copyright © 1996, 2004, 2007, 2013 by Tyndale House Foundation. Used by permission of Tyndale House Publishers Inc., Carol Stream, Illinois 60188. All rights reserved.

All rights reserved. No part of this publication may be reproduced, stored in a retrieval system, or transmitted in any form or by any means—electronic, mechanical, photocopy, recording, or any other—except for brief quotations in printed reviews, without the prior permission of the publisher or author, except as provided by USA copyright law.

Printed in the United States of America

Dedicated to

My precious granddaughter,
Annamarie Joy
and
Our precious Savior,
Jesus the Christ

Who is Jesus?

Is he someone who takes your favorite teddy bear?

No. Jesus doesn't take your favorite teddy bear.
Jesus gives you His teddy bear.

For God loved the world so much
that he gave his one and only Son,
so that everyone who believes in him
will not perish but have eternal life.

~ John 3:16

Who is Jesus?

Is he someone who laughs at you when you fall down and hurt yourself?

No. Jesus doesn't laugh at you when you fall down and hurt yourself. Jesus picks you up, brushes you off, and gives you a big hug.

*But you, O Lord,
are a God of compassion and mercy.*

~ Psalm 86:15

Who is Jesus?

Is he someone who pushes you away when it's time to play hide-and-seek?

No. Jesus doesn't push you away when it's time to play hide-and-seek. Jesus NEVER pushes you away. He wants to be your friend. Your BEST friend

"You are my friends,
if you do what I command."

~ John 15:14

Who is Jesus?

Is he someone who gives you a tummy ache when you've been naughty?

No. Jesus doesn't give you a tummy ache when you've been naughty.
Jesus NEVER gives you a tummy ache.
Jesus takes away your tummy ache.

*He forgives all my sins
and heals all my diseases.*

~ Psalm 103:3

Who is Jesus?

Is he someone who yells at you when you cry?

God is our refuge and strength,
always ready to help in times of trouble.

~ Psalm 46:1

Who is Jesus?

Is he someone who leaves you behind when you are lost in the mall?

No. Jesus doesn't leave you behind when you are lost in the mall. Jesus always knows where you are, and He will take care of you.

"For the Son of Man came to seek and save those who are lost."

~ Luke 19:10

Who is Jesus?

Is he someone who stops loving you when you do something wrong?

*And I am convinced that
nothing can ever separate us from God's love.*

~ Romans 8:38

Who is Jesus?

God is love.
~ 1 John 4:8

Jesus is Love.

Who is Jesus?

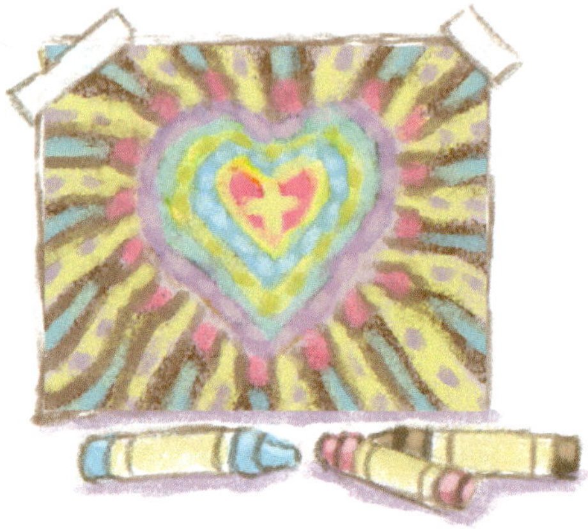

Jesus is GOD!

"The Father and I are one."
~ John 10:30

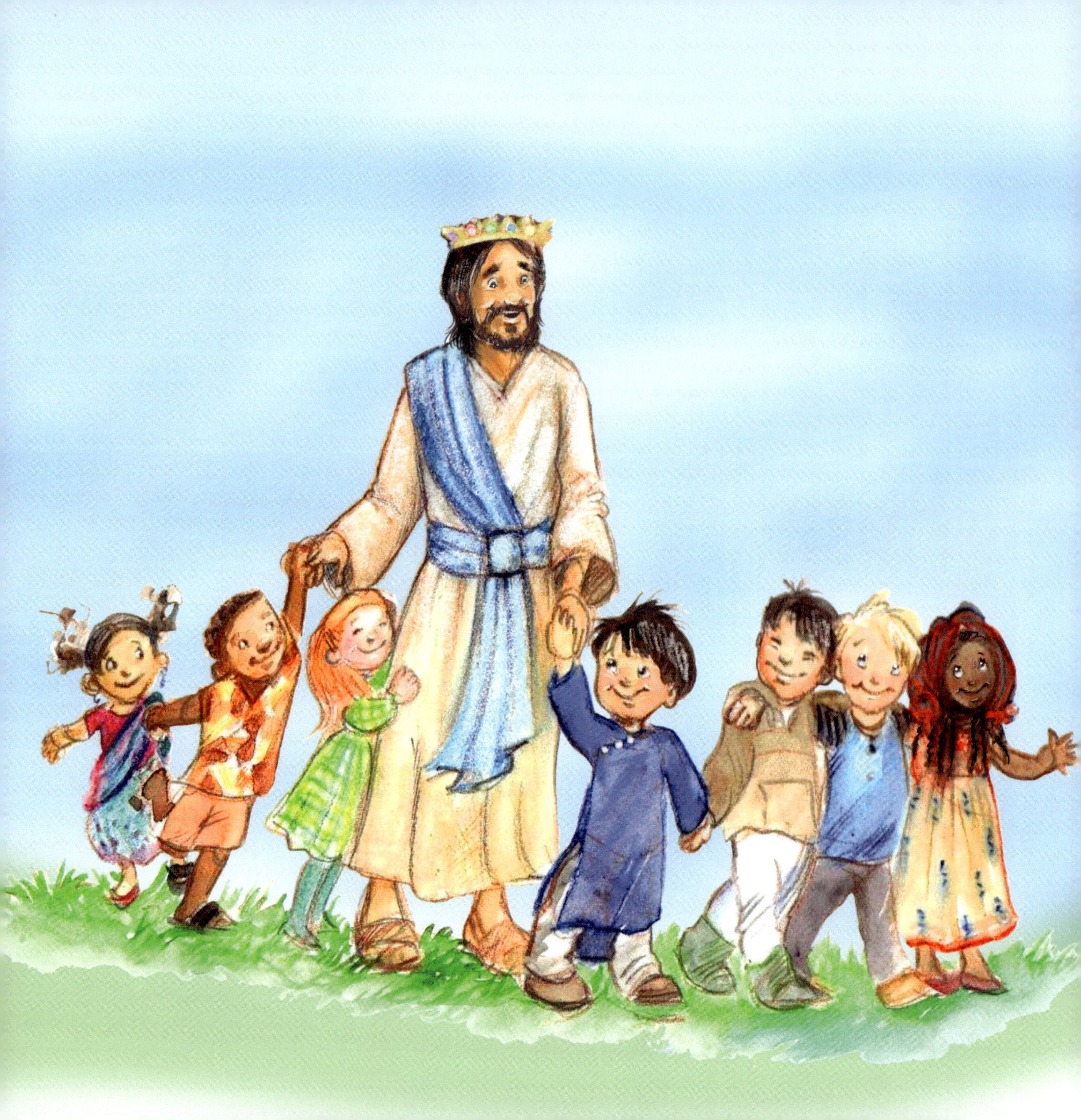

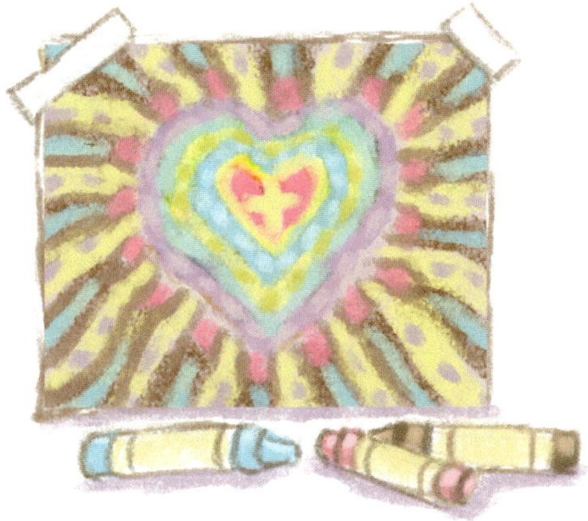

Meet the Author
MaryAnn Diorio

Dr. MaryAnn Diorio earned her PhD in French from the University of Kansas and her MFA in Writing Popular Fiction from Seton Hill University. She is a diplomate of the Institute of Children's Literature and has taught writing at Rowan University and Regent University. Her stories for children have appeared in numerous magazines. Dr. MaryAnn, as she is affectionately called, resides in New Jersey with her husband Dom. They are blessed with two awesome daughters, a wonderful son-in-law, and a precious granddaughter. When she is not writing stories, MaryAnn loves to paint, to read, and to make up silly songs for little Annamarie.

Visit MaryAnn at www.maryanndiorio.com.

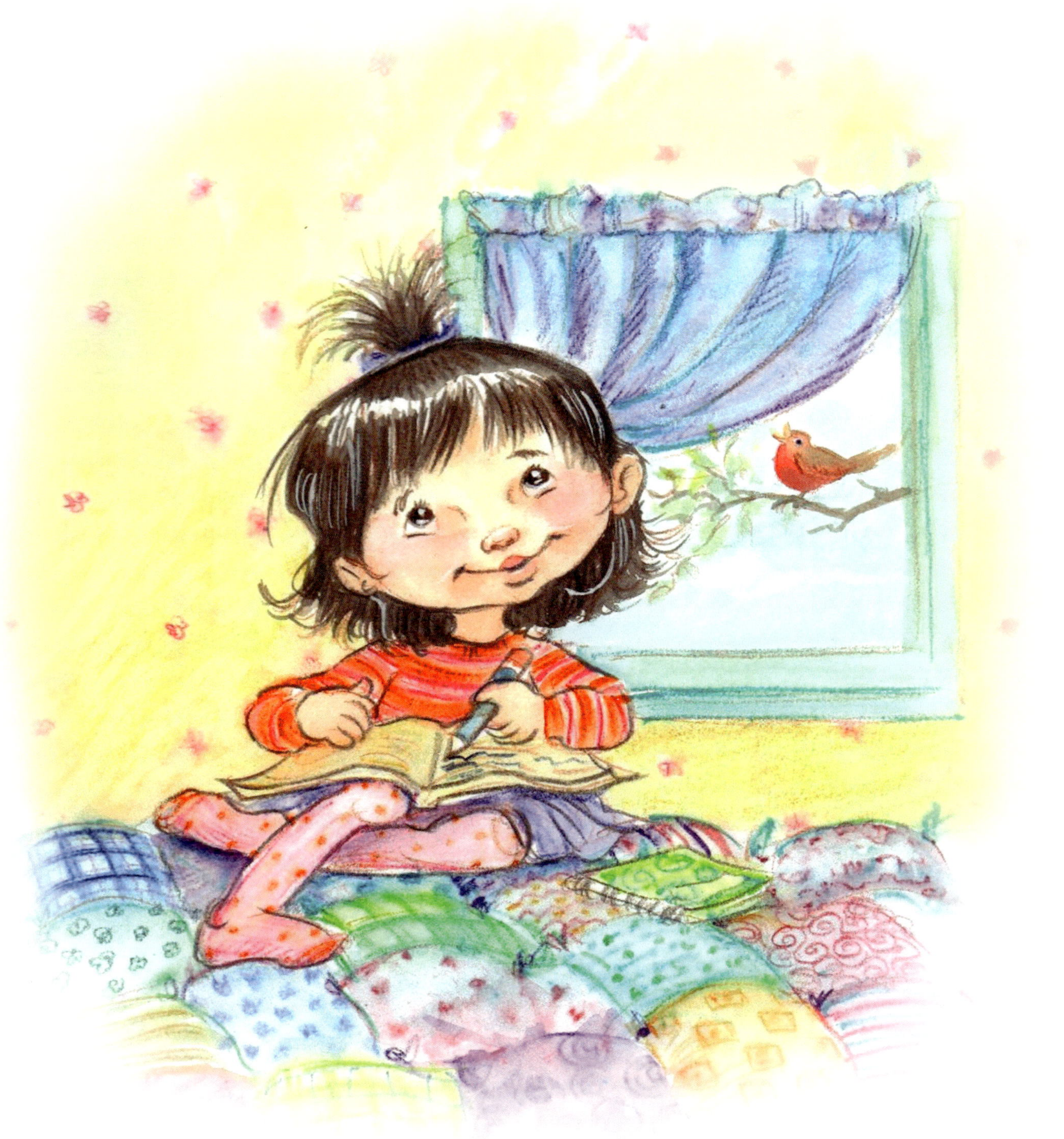

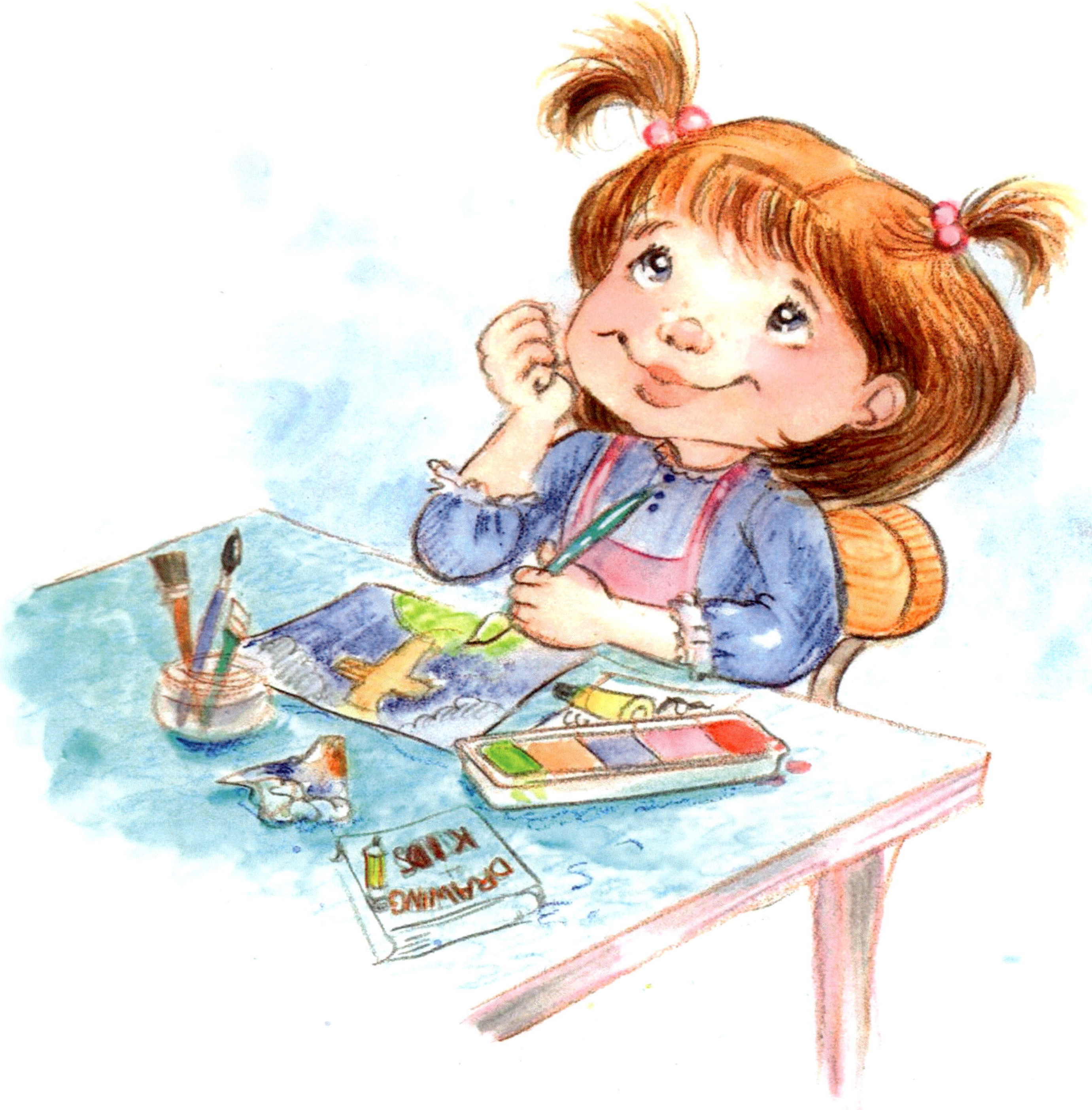
DRAWING
KIDS

meet the Illustrator
Kim Sponaugle

Kim Sponaugle is a children's book illustrator. Upon graduation from The Art Institute of Philadelphia, she began working for DC Cook Publishing as an associate designing children's curriculum, but soon found her heart vocation in children's illustration. While working as a kid's portrait artist, Kim developed a style that captured the effervescence of childhood and has tried to incorporate that joy into her book work. In 2007, Kim started Picture Kitchen Studio and has since had the opportunity and pleasure of illustrating more than fifty books for kids. Picture Kitchen Studio has been honored to receive the Mom's Choice, Pinnacle Book, CIPA EVVY and Reader's Favorite Awards.

Visit Kim at www.picturekitchenstudio.com.

Who is Jesus?

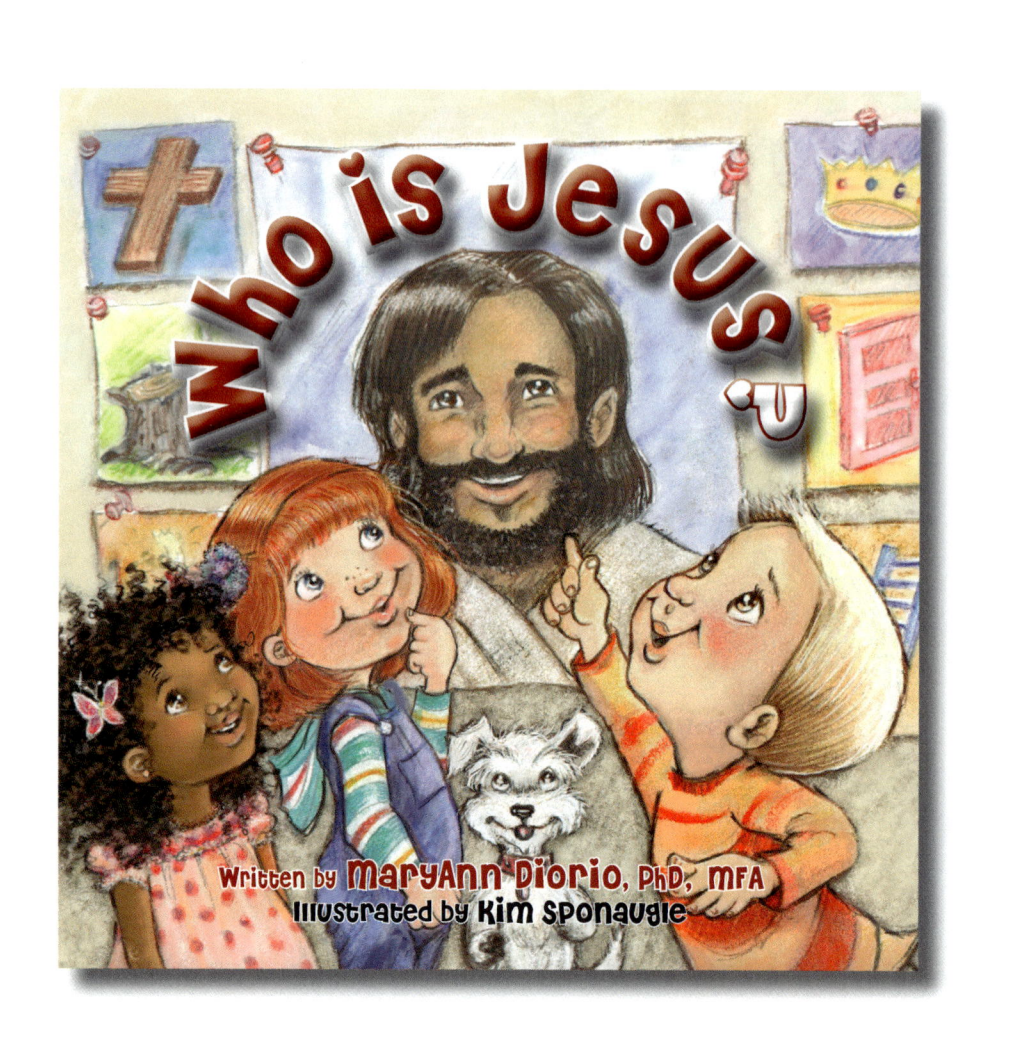

Written by MaryAnn Diorio, PhD, MFA
Illustrated by Kim Sponaugle

To Order

Visit www.maryanndiorio.com
For autographed books or to schedule speaking engagements,

contact MaryAnn at 856.488.3580
or e-mail at info@topnotchpress.com

www.TopNotchPress.com

Discounts available through the publisher
for bulk orders and fundraisers:

Published by TopNotch Press
PO Box 1185, Merchantville, NJ 08109
P: 856-488-3580 - F: 856-488-0291
www.topnotchpress.com
info@topnotchpress.com

Also available wherever books are sold.

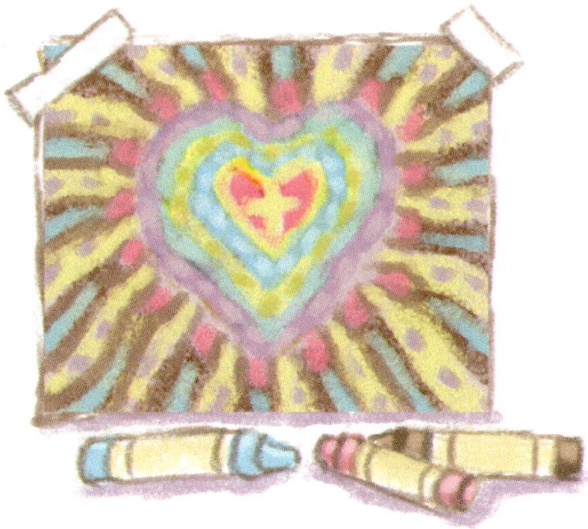